DEFENSIVE RAPTURE

BOOKS BY BARBARA GUEST

*The Location of Things* (Tibor de Nagy, 1960)
*Poems: The Location of Things; Archaics;*
*The Open Skies* (Doubleday & Company, 1962)
*The Blue Stairs* (Corinth Books, 1968)
*Moscow Mansions* (Viking, 1973)
*The Countess from Minneapolis* (Burning Deck, 1976)
*Seeking Air* (fiction) (Black Sparrow, 1977)
*The Türler Losses* (Montréal: Mansfield Book Mart, 1979)
*Biography* (Burning Deck, 1980)
*Herself Defined: The Poet H.D. and Her World* (biography)
(Doubleday & Company, 1984)
*Musicality* (Kelsey Street Press, 1988)
*Fair Realism* (Sun & Moon Press, 1989)
*Defensive Rapture* (Sun & Moon Press, 1993)

# Defensive Rapture

BARBARA GUEST

SUN &
MOON

CLASSICS

30

Sun & Moon Press
A Program of The Contemporary Arts Educational Project, Inc.
a nonprofit corporation
6026 Wilshire Boulevard, Los Angeles, California 90036

This edition first published in paperback in 1993 by Sun & Moon Press
10 9 8 7 6 5 4 3 2 1
FIRST EDITION

This book was made possible, in part, through a operational grant from the
Andrew W. Mellon Foundation and through contributions to
The Contemporary Arts Educational Project, Inc.,
a nonprofit corporation
Some of these poems previously appeared in
*The American Poetry Review, Blue Mesa, Conjunctions, Hambone,
New American Writing, O.blēk, Sulfur,* and *Temblor.*
*The Altos,* with art by Richard Tuttle, was printed by
Hank Hine Editions, 1991.
The author wishes to thank the editors of these publications.

*Cover:* Photograph by Seton Smith
Reprinted by permission of the artist

LIBRARY OF CONGRESS CATALOGING IN PUBLICATION DATA

Guest, Barbara (1920)
Defensive Rapture
p. cm — (Sun & Moon Classics: 30)
ISBN: 1-55713-032-9
I. Title. II. Series.
811'.54—dc20

Printed in the United States of America on acid-free paper.

# TABLE OF CONTENTS

| | |
|---|---|
| Paulownia | 9 |
| Dove | 13 |
| Expectation | 20 |
| Geese Blood | 23 |
| *Fleet of White* | 27 |
| Atmospheres | 30 |
| The Surface as Object | 34 |

## II

| | |
|---|---|
| Defensive Rapture | 41 |
| Beautiful/Evil | 44 |
| Borrowed Mirror, Filmic Rise | 46 |
| Restlessness | 47 |
| Chalk | 51 |

## III

| | |
|---|---|
| Borderlands | 61 |
| Dissonance Royal Traveller | 64 |
| The Advance of the Grizzly | 70 |
| The Glass Mountain | 73 |
| Otranto | 80 |
| Winter Horses | 87 |

## IV

| | |
|---|---|
| The Altos | 93 |

*To Perdita*

# Paulownia

### i

ravenous the still dark a fishnet—
    robber walk near formidable plaits
    a glaze—the domino overcast—


seized by capes—budding splash
whitened—with strokes—
        silvertone gravure.
            knifed tree.



straw beneficence—
                ambient cloud. riderless.


### ii

vowels inclement—tossed off figure
    lisping blot—
            running figure.
            bowled ripe.
    stood in the wind sheet. a fermur axis.
        virginal wail. as grain. storm motif.

iii

pierced the risen sea.
   coxcomb.
slides around.

       day and night.

      "remedy of darkness"
       lit body.


iv

etched in powder

sequence—a solace

    the monument.
   width of grape—is praised.

v

adherence to sand
the loam division—the quagmire


foot sink the rind—
    or    rindswift heel
astonished acre
        chewed wire.



vi

as instrument

    threaded sky
    burnt.
torn from the corner.
on your knees



vii

plinth in sour bloom.

the idiot cone. rummage.

viii

held     in mortar air.

'weight of stone'

    fragment.


ix

their whole selves—
    or were they?

burden of face
    from one to the other


   *quaking sun.*

     *abstract arm.*

# Dove

experienced in rounded

dove form

belly up the child toy

anointed.

other codes—

like granite where the toy

the ground submissive—

splays

lightness under curled vapor.

"we wear open clothes.

and we are

broken up into time intervals."

one day bridges.

neophytes passing over.  three vans.

flight of open sticks.

waving.




repeated—

as idiom—

"their fear of absorption—

a common scale."


what is printed—

determinant lion

as music—;


ordinary leaves

estranged—proportionate wind—

felled.

and plots of sandust.

"the thing that was dear"—

        scenes with table.


      an intense

idolizing.      frame with multiple rose.




      sunset

      venom in rust

       the small breathing.

of cowhide.


      employed

a chalk wing.

      the globular

solitude

invisible swell

"touching the beyond"

has no body without another.

walless.

at the nib—dove shunted downward;

survives—in buoyant leap

admits the crater lump—the advance

performs more violently as violent solution

picks up speed

outside of character

outside the dovecote—

a rascallion soar          multi-layered emotional

suffix.

"he may never know why"

The scribbling

dynamic—skewed

meter shift      the merging

print and tense

range of cardboard

dominant

*papier peint*

flat ink transcribes:

"the patterned brilliance

through open doors"

*on foraged studio cloud*

*the painted raven*

feeds the hermit bread.

the whinnied pupil scratch      anxious

from the stalk ear the eye reached up and the

sublimated eye reroutes the gaze

world of trout    a neutralized shape

the portal earth threw    toad gaze

on

mottled dove

water outside the spoon.

# Expectation

(Ewartung: Schœnberg)


more liquid
than eyes adulterous surface—

the bruised arch—a sting
severely clothed—rich in dynamite—
cord to shallows—;

a fluid haze divides—
the rhythm vault—

—single movement—topped with purple hills—
contralto shift—.

———————

*variations*

masked throat—

gradual broken ascent
—means intensify

through an aperture—the tilt

grave—
ropings.

      —they flutter—pick on straw

      tinted bird
band around the slender hollow—
      tight noise—rolled


      —of itself
smoke white regal     chromatic rise
     of itself
       unattached.

-------------------

     pieces laid
placement vital to
         disguise.

    the basilic    arrangement
      in view

      unaffected

     leaning on elbows

-------------------

tumescent—whitened girders—the spatial breath—

delicate mouthing—a pain hesitancy—

the tread of corn husk—aural sky—

                  between inheritances—;

brevity emphasized—an unnatural heart beat—

without the nominative curve—

to be grasped—the wooden handle

                  diminished—;

   a gravelly endless pact—

littered octave—disrupted—

knee bound—mutinied—spells the translucent.

## Geese Blood

height of trees

the papered chamber—

a breathy click—low volumed—

the stalking men—

outer motions

leading to holes—unstable lacing—

an elevation—

controlled surface—

seizures—the fallow lining—

a bird interrupts—

groping for layers—

lip fold—

loosed on the hillside—                    dun panorama

continues a secondary

reliance on ledge—the nearest forest—reversed

kilometres—a brusque rim—the outer motion—

as figurative—

extension of features—

leading to holes—an elevated fissure;

these intervals control—

in bold gaps—marked by flaking—The empty lining—

The bird in fallow sky—the motion

exits into forest shelter—

the lighter than expected—height of trees—

aware the figure

now withdrawn in commotive patterns—agitates

low volume—men stalking—the open visor—

ruffled leaves

held with cotton—gloves—in pursuit of sunlight—

the raw bloom—polarized—

tunneling.

the ace spring—          an inch into—

mosaic.

eye bell—

a mirror dice—                    an opening.

sand bowls in—

cotton gloves—

two hunting knives—

the dried-up glint—


spirit guide—

under three arches—green hand.          sunken bowls.

'red geese blood'.

## Fleet of White

i

coming into the park

through the white magnolias—

only those eyes 'veiled'—

saw Syracuse.

*'Scipio's tomb*

*contains no ashes now.'*

ii

piece of cloth in evening storm

sideways into air

mullion glow

'hugging' the shore

flute-like barque

wash of quarter-tones.

iii

*arranged*

*on the same level*

*figures*

*on a dusty shoulder*

*move to another level.*

*'stuff of*        *dream'*

*mistakes for*       *shift in place*

                 *return and fade.*

*Fleet of White.*

## Atmospheres

faster—than the stare

        —salutary—ornamental bruising;

the ellipsis—a thin ring—

precedes thunder—triggered—heathery

discipline—lining up—unshakeable granite—

the normal morass—green and white mix—

above the sea crop

settled—and retrieved the skin—vocable

dust-skeined—rim—

fence proof—firm date—the uprising—

the quartered horse—from tree to dowser—

torrent clad—in night pathetic.

dog quickness—in the burned-out tertiary—

the grimace—a nerve fault—;

                    combined ochreous—

   hesitancy—tumbling—the marsh period—

        sod—mounted antlers the common

dark—murmurs— —unheated—stoic ground


            —burst with the imaginary shadowless

crawls—;

        domination by modal

        alliance of moves—sculptured

weighing—the tube circuits slicked—

                out of sky.

in widow—field—to establish multiple erasures—

a plain mobility—diatonic—released cloud cuttings—

a simplex—within the marginal

                —giant originals.

squeezed—from memory the ash zones—collective ritual—

astronomic mood power—into memory pushed—

a piping reservoir—elemental softening—subliminal


as through the stations—in astral grip—

intravenous search through structured—visible—

faulting—the loud test—a slowed metabolic—

release—chaff filters


the disease pattern—mirror particle—;

under the skin—a loss of time—

under the heroic—memory cap—retains the wall—

the thickness mined—

levitation—passage.


to the stick road—to the track—

hurt—in the narrow—shoulder

passed—the threshold—lightning giblets—after the

burning—the crossfire—

                tied—thrust outside

primitive method—conjured—

diamonds into the hand.

## The Surface as Object

the visible

as in the past

subsisting in layered zone

refuses to dangle

oaths on marsh field

whitened or planned

memorial distance

rather than vine

that which proliferates

the bittersweet grapple

                initiates

        a mysterious mesh

forbids    the instant disclosure

        delays a humid course

or creates a patina

        jungleware.


or she moving forward into

the line of sticks

        circled by sticks

her hand flies up

        in the direct line of sticks

odor of lines.

knowing the difficulty

annexation of Egypt

     oaths on marsh fields etc.


       a possible intimacy with

the tomblike fragrance of stone

       the cult-like

expressiveness.


       (the perpendicular

millimeter stone

     less raw


  or, gangling

as the artful

lessening surprised.)

tree grown guava

oaths on marsh field

the hungry minstrel and the forager

gold on the guava lick of rosin

and the chill latched thicket

grunt marsh weed

*regardez-la*

the untamed ibis.

II

# Defensive Rapture

Width of a cube spans defensive rapture
cube from blocks of liquid theme
phantom of lily stark
in running rooms.


adoration of hut performs a clear function
illusive column extending dust
protective screen the red
objects pavilion.


deep layered in tradition moonlight
folkloric pleads the rakish
sooted idiom
supernatural diadem.


stilled grain of equinox
turbulence the domicile
host robed arm white
crackled motives.

sensitive timbre with complex
astral sign open tent hermetic
toss of sand swan reeds
torrents of uneveness.


surround a lusted fabric
hut sequence modal shy
as verdigris hallow force
massive intimacy.


slant fuse the wived
mosaic a chamber astrakhan
amorous welding
the sober descant.


turns in the mind bathes
the rapture bone a guardian
ploy indolent lighted
strew of doubt.


commends internal habitude
bush the roof
day stare gliding
double measures.

qualms the weights of night
medusæ raft clothed sky
radiant strike the oars
skim cirrus.


evolve a fable husk
aged silkiness the roan
planet mowed like ears
beaded grip.


suppose the hooded grass
numb moat alum trench a solemn
glaze the sexual estuary
floats an edge.

## Beautiful/Evil

fifteen diamonds in a row

and one red

       "ruby"

brought down the gravel—in lumps.


out of the fire orphanage—

       with a carpet bag.


       "celestial essence"

all-gifted.       *Pandora.*

owlish—the lifted eyebrows—

Minerva-like.

wrapped in a bird coat

*geworfen*

"hurled into existence"

breathed into.

beautiful/evil.

## Borrowed Mirror, Filmic Rise

Arriving speeds the chromatic
we stay with fire

arrows jasper pontifex declare
an imaginative risk.

fermented moss a
bulge in aramanth

motley filmic rise
that welds a natural

shield refreshed in hutch
of oak.

from borrowed mirror
rain a seized and

crystal pruner the limned
and eyed cowl

eyedusk.

# Restlessness

## 1

    oh conscript not the forest
a stone and laughter

    it sports a halo
filled with drops one after the other

in the efficacious zone they fall like minerals

and the courtesans move to a narrow spot
where their lids are tinted and the slight
huskiness of

a cat's mouth enters.

## 2

*it was when I stayed with her that I first heard the sound of
violin and piano and orchestra…*

in that part of the forest these instruments wcre unknown
…the first 'scent' of the West.

3

he swims holding the wood handle
eyes smudged below the iris
burned leaves thrown from her fingers

wildlife running from the edge
four persons inside a hut
a passage from the shared bowl
throwing the rind outside the bowl.

grown ups working in the forest
tidying hair at the car window
noodles, plasticity.

4

now they move through indigo
the shape of their shoulder
armpit
even the bag of garnets
they rave about steals from
dark blue and they

wish to copulate
in that medium
hands in the noodles

wayfare in shadow city.


5


    a lantern
among the grasses
    smoke from white lanterns;

yonder the corpse
wrapped in straw.

insect voices
    filtering through the woodcut

upon the tombstone the last
poem of *Takahashi O-den*

    oh the straw hunchedness.

even the willow
vanished from Tama River

the shivering flavor
disappeared.

naphtha on her skin.

when he stays with her
'the violins the piano and orchestra'

the western 'scent.'

---

italics on page 47: Hasegawa Shigure

# Chalk

i

*you await assumptions induced by temperament—*

ecclesiastic in wing power—

narrow abridgement    yellow slanders the island

lavable breeze work.

the catalogue within the visor—

reticule of mannerists.   employable objects.

minor tenses born in the scrubs—

irregular

flame—

exiled   grass.

ii

voiceless Etruria

the mythic quarry—

*fireball tunneled.*

jovial stone   cipherless—

hijacked.   lively.


iii

with eyecatch—

on rocks off Scylla

silvered goats entering.   leaving.


Memory plunge.   tossed.   refined.

post-attic rhythms juggled.

in beggar garb Odysseus

—the Cyclops pinched like rose plums.


*'steals    memory'*


brittle nosed.

shuttle loom.



iv

1.

unfashionable—

bent at the waist.   professional at descendant hour—

*vase galop*

unarmored amid

glued piecework   impotent   vessel—

Thracian meld.

skidded root power.

2.

a fairly simple footwork

the body painted white—

*an air of decay*    in the toothless pattern

light in controlled areas—lavender extensions—

the chambers tied into bundles

says the body.

an oiled leap

embracing the skin    minimal in shyness

circling—crumpling—rising

the six scenes.


cricket music for the robing.


v

the Orphic rite film releases


bathybius


miniature displacement.   mountain   dialect partial.

(ph formally silent)

indices proper to songster.


zephyrstorm and flute—


*heroic spin beneath subsoil*—


regal smiles.   conversation shaded—


black currant tin.

vi

a half root elasticized

the upright valve a harpsichord

in steel diminuendo    *historicism*—

alabaster hooded—

reduces complex Medea—the narrow unbridled hand—:

"mere      antique queen"

*aisle of lopped off heads*


vii

little is missing even plumped shadow—

a knight observes his dress—

under the rough mountain

tree growth out of rock.

*a natural tone in the poems.*

lid pried open    volumes fall out—


lightning sinks into soft thunder and

weights of earth balance.


viii

a slice paradisical

flickers into melted *jaune*


astrew the careless Arcadian—

red-tiled slumber.  dowerless.


the waxed emptiness—moulting stone—

agrarian fable.

III

# Borderlands

The return was like a snowbird like the cutoff

    before the orchard we remembered;

they came to us as rustlers

        the steeds were foam.


The girl in the bonnet the man with shoulder pads

were familiar the rustic was anyone's choice

he chortled; there was mutual glee

        it clammered.


    Welcome in a new fashion a century had passed

    bones tucked away even wreaths

        headbands

    where orchards joined an isthmus was winter.

Our preoccupation began with grass hoeing when

it starts to roam, folding down corners

watching the tubular form;

desiring no money we were

serene like a nation.


We shifted our feet, tribal

at desolate speech or,

canoeing a worn river,

fought separately when they held us up;

why is this remembered, how is it explained?


"Escape with me!"

we hear them say and look at the drivelling

margin at the inch where stone refused to burn

light on rural habitation.

You cannot tell them what glass resembles they

skid on the track;

reindeer eat moss

the subject is not the assassin.

*Lands incorporated by the Treaty of Versailles in 1919 to form
Czechoslovakia: Bohemia, Moravia, Silesia, Slovakia, Ruthenia.

# Dissonance Royal Traveller

sound opens sound

shank of  globe                    strings floating out

*something like images are here*

opening up avenues to view a dome

a distant clang reaches the edifice.

*understanding what it means*
*to understand music*

cloudless movement   beyond the neck's reach

an hypnotic lull in porcelain   water break   mimics

tonality   crunch of sand under waddling

>*a small seizure*
>*from monumentality*

>does not come or go   with understanding

the path will end

birdhouse   of trembling cotton

or dream   expelled it

parcel   on the landlocked moor.

*explaining music*

and their clothes entangled

who walk into a puddle of minnows;

minnows in a bowl

consonant with water.

the drifted footpad

ambushed by reeds signals the listening

oars.

music disappears into oars.

in the middle the world is brown;

on the opposite side of the earth

an aroma of scarlet.

this accompanies our hearing music;

the sleeve of heaven

and the hoof of earth

loosed from their garrison.

dissonance may abandon *miserere*

on bruised knee hasten to the idol.

and what is consonance—the recluse—

entering and exiting

as often as a monarch butterfly

touches a season;

by accident grips the burning flowers.

in the stops between terror

the moon aflame on its plaza.

autumn of rippling wind

and the noise of baskets

smell of tin fists.


and harsh fists

on the waterfall changing the season;

the horse romps in flax

a cardboard feature

creating a cycle of flax.


*music imagines this cardboard*

the horse in cardboard jacket

      flagrant the ragged grove

            red summit red.

    dissonance royal traveller

            altered the red saddle.

## The Advance of the Grizzly

go from the must-laden room

move to the interior

the remarkable bird in the case;

       wing

(like a pillow).


bird out of cloud—dissembling of trees; locks;

the icicle; out of the margin


falling from the grim margin the axle of skin;

enamoured with the fell wing.


I will move in my skin with the hollow

the neck and the brimming over the latitude

over the latitude onto the brink.

frame of snow "within

squares of diminishing size"

ink hushed the snow; a blank sky rolled to the verge

parable heaved through drift...

and the moon weighted

with this the coil


evoked our willing to believe in a sudden pull

of the immense frame at the heel:


spilled exactly

to destroy a circular return

from the ragged prose clump

clump on the cold landscape


white grown fatter... place of sharpened skin.

romantic fever and snow

fresh from the gorgon bed

    *dendrophagous* "feeding on trees"

to sustain the romantic vision route over snow

the sudden drop into pines:


    "feeding on trees"

new mouths red of Okeechobee.


(and ate the alligator and spat out the part

wedded to the green clavicle.)


loss of the sun


blight of the sun the looney forest

who will walk out of the plush interior into

the excited atmosphere?


an outlet for prose the advance of the grizzly.

# The Glass Mountain

*in memory of J.S.*

i

king as wanderer

replied     we do and always

the least recounting

pelting dew

bird in the sunrise room;

once or twice the landscape burns

what we are after tires

clouds mohair.

rhododendron bring

pods to the mountain;

a tremulous position

harp on a mountain of glass.

ii

is it a power

you pass in the night

taking water from the tap,

fog or phantom

the king stares at.

you are not the snake lady

gold filament above

the snake limbs

nor does she tell

who taught the dance.

iii

the king watched

in flat country the

caravan at ewe season

a density

sand and thyme

near the threshold

where they milk

have bitten the nut-

like substance

bauble of sound

mahogany the king


travelling the length

overhead a climate

of twang the rushed snow


unstoppable space in the bold

different in the next imagined

movement the breach


is inimitable

a phrase others believe

there is no escape


the towed rock dims.

v

    why not live

         image strewn

and goes pitter pat

next to the resolute corridor

and a diadem would hang on the fringe

actual pieces of tame fibre shut off.


on the steeple with the watercan

and thunder in the earring she

caught the speech of the termagant

the roll


was seen the plummage and owl

a raft on the cold river; skin

on the raft a king

picked up boards and sunk them.

vi

the shades lavished

in the ideal

climate of planets fear

steam rolling up;

holding hands in a ring

wet to their waists

          hair

a slippery blossom.

exposure beneath the May apse

         doggerel;

chunks of filched

         objects not

lapidary; a king.

attent on detail

    the hullabaloo over

rule half water half worn

    running the notion of land;


tells us where light comes from

    white curtains in its beak;

closer closer to the splintered mountain


O king endlessly

scattering.

# Otranto

At sunset from the top of the stair watching

the castle mallets wrenched from their socket

fell from ambush into flame flew into hiding;

above the stoneware a latch like muscle hid

the green; he stood waist high under the rapt

ceiling and hanged the sparrow; where the kitchen

had been a mirror of eggs served in a tumbler he

saw the ring when a lancet pierced and threw it.

In a basket and lowered it where sails enter

the harbor over a parchment like dominoes;

the petrel-like eyelash.

To the sun and its rites were pulled the dried

banners; they flew past the ruins the tower

and window where ivory guided the mist on his back;

he rubbed his eyes and counted them kneeling

wrinkled as grass.

*A ghost in their nostrils put a heel at their*

*forehead; they saw only the moon as it*

*fasted.*

ii

If the ship meant anything if he heard a world

view in the midst of his rhythm or the spell

lustrous like hair on his arm; that groaned as

it struck near the tumble down or

combing hair; words burnt as they quickened.

*The bitter they share crept into forage and*

*muster is in their skin; the grey*

*worked like a vise they brushed this*

*to turn arrows; they shut off the vast*

*cellar and the turret leaped to a pattern;*

*the mosaic blended was untouched.*

### iii

The frankish hills and hummocks metered

the greed over sun and cloud; voluptuous

in the straits turbanned held scarves to the

water each sail embroidered;

who washed in their music a lattice.

*A major or borrowed sky this aspect provides*

*the lily stalk inside the frame; a gesture the lily*

*pointing north as if the wrench from sky decides*

*cold rain or change of tide; the lily*

*she chooses.*


iv

Waking in must the high pierced window dew on

the furnaced bar the poaching hour the cup

takes smoke from the tower; they drink

in the smoke the print cradled; cut in dark.


*The siege made cloth a transfer*

*learned from invaders who craved it;*

*spindle thieves.*

She sang high notes and pebbles went into her

work where it changed into marks; in that room

the armor-like wrens:


rites turned with thread a dower

begs lapis; eglantine on a spoon; the castle

breeds tallow.


v


A change of tide might delay the run

they watched as if by simple water

read magisterially whatever the book decided;

*night outside covered with filmic screen*

*ghosts they store; then bring an experimental*

*wheel out of hiding.*

Even the Nile wind; fortune cards

jugglers a remedy from old clothes;

to appease the fable—pearls

rolling in straw.


The way a cowslip bends

they remember or Troilus as he stared;

they agree on brighter covers; looser

shifts fluent tower to tower.


More ephemeral than roundness or

the grown pear tree connected

with vision a rose briar.

*There was only a rugged footpath*

*above the indifferent straits and a shelf where the*

*castle lay perhaps it was sphered like Otranto;*

*there the traveller stood naked and talked*

*aloud or found a lily and thought a sword;*

*or dragged a carcass upon blunt stone like a*

*corded animal. In weeds in spiritual*

*seclusion a felt hand lifted.*

## Winter Horses

placed two sticks upon a dazzling plate

unlike feudal wars you remember

their saying she is stalking

and the fortifications are blocked

abruptly they held their breath until it froze.


carpeting the greensward a foil of sunset

"idyll of the kings" and shut the moat;

did not forget the promised tawny

situation of splendor.


again twists in the passage

or is it rhythm overturned;

to regard moodily a cask something

borrowed or fable stuck the snow.

ii

sea grey cold a door one boulder

slams another.

      instantly footprints

in the sand corner.


      grief spell was thought something else

records what was cried out.

the shrived warm

      turns into serpent

        are

no kingdoms

      is grass.

iii

winter

you know how it is *la gloire!*

       they bring you a fig dish.

the dead in white cotton.

fleece on the platter.

       wind crept

the white shoat and buried;

the cramped space ran

       out of breathing.

iv

bars of snow lanced the brightness

crippled windows flung

lute with two notes unevenly.

ice breaking and noise

envelops sobriety.

slice of boot on the frayed sylph

came out of dazzlement into

fisheries was intended.

IV

# The Altos

… the warbler

      where did he locate the bell

      … has crossed the river

        field plane

     table of     syllabic     water

              out of rock

     moved backward

     in floated matinal

chimera

     rests his eyes.

circle    lavender

of

in the tide region

modular lope.

'located harbors'

rice in autumn

*emplastos* over the signet

'papered halo'

to walk somewhere

an image falls

out of the figurative sky

offers what bell it is.

from the walk   voice asks   whose

covered walk from

the past     a white satchel

the embonpoint

is sacred        mortar

on the threshold

beside the ragged dome

dust lips

running it cannot stop

it falls into segmentary rushes


narrow gauntlet

a slipper untied it.


with staff     the bony road

came toward us

pallor of grey harbor

bird eye of the Altos

from open green to take the purest juice

it strengthens the turbans

the braided helmet said 'mine mine'

heir to evening arches

oh the ace of evening

butterfly      on the night drop

across the pavement

viols

call to mates

balloon smell

with the tiger

an invisible weight

swam in the

night          into thunder

cannot find

the platinum

bird coat

dreamed the stalk image

a gestural branch

lily powdered

distance

in baking dew

with full hands

with many branches


coldest butter


alive in the coal meadow


tipped the grief-scale

an antic of wild

deposition—raincoats dripping—

romantic barriers—


they believe the staged cloud—

even the fountain of Altos


their soft meats cross the border.

# BARBARA GUEST

Born in North Carolina, Barbara Guest spent her childhood in California and Florida. After graduating from the University of California at Berkeley, she settled in New York City.

Guest was connected with the group of poets later known as the New York Poets. During the 1960s she published *The Location of Things, Poems, The Blue Stairs*. An attachment to art found in her poetry was formed when she began to write for *Art News* and other art journals.

*Moscow Mansions* (1973), *The Countess from Minneapolis* (1976), and, in particular her novel, *Seeking Air* (1978), point to a sense of structure more varied and experimental as her poetics step outside the frame of the knighthood of the New York School.

Work on *Herself Defined,* Guest's 1984 acclaimed biography of the poet H.D., consumed five years, during which time Guest published only one book of poetry. When in 1989 *Fair Realism* was published by Sun & Moon Press and received the Lawrence Lipton Award for Literature, it was noted her dependence on language, always a variant, now placed her closer physically to the Language poets, and it was clear that there she was more at ease, although sharing an unsubsidized tenancy.

Robert Long in reviewing *Fair Realism* seizes on her "unique capacity to pull the reader through a series of linguistic veils, her unpredictability, her ongoing attempt to define what representation—what realism—is." He writes that Guest "moves the reader from one level of comprehension to another, from the easily accessible to the more obscure. Reading a Guest poem, one is reminded again and again of the surface of the poem—of language's transparencies as well as its inscrutabilities."

# SUN & MOON CLASSICS

The Sun & Moon Classics is a publicly supported, nonprofit program to publish new editions and translations or republications of outstanding world literature of the late nineteenth and twentieth centuries. Through its publication of living authors as well as great masters of the century, the series attempts to redefine what usually is meant by the idea of a "classic" by dehistoricizing the concept and embracing a new, ever changing literary canon.

Organized by the Contemporary Arts Educational Project, Inc., a nonprofit corporation, and published by its program Sun & Moon Press, the series is made possible, in part, by grants and individual contributions.

This book was made possible, in part, through a matching grant from the National Endowment for the Arts, from the California Arts Council, through an organizational grant from the Andrew W. Mellon Foundation, and through contributions from the following individuals:

Charles Altieri (Seattle, Washington)
John Arden (Galway, Ireland)
Dennis Barone (West Hartford, Connecticut)
Jonathan Baumbach (Brooklyn, New York)
Bill Berkson (Bolinas, California)
Steve Benson (Berkeley, California)
Sherry Bernstein (New York, New York)
Bill Corbett (Boston, Massachusetts)
Fielding Dawson (New York, New York)
Robert Crosson (Los Angeles, California)
Tina Darragh and P. Inman (Greenbelt, Maryland)
Christopher Dewdney (Toronto, Canada)
Philip Dunne (Malibu, California)
George Economou (Norman, Oklahoma)
Elaine Equi and Jerome Sala (New York, New York)
Lawrence Ferlinghetti (San Francisco, California)
Richard Foreman (New York, New York)
Howard N. Fox (Los Angeles, California)
Jerry Fox (Aventura, Florida)
In Memoriam: Rose Fox
Melvyn Freilicher (San Diego, California)

# BOOKS IN THE SUN & MOON CLASSICS SERIES

1 Gertrude Stein *Mrs. Reynolds*

2 Djuna Barnes *Smoke and Other Early Stories*

3 Stijn Streuvels *The Flaxfield** 

4 Marianne Hauser *Prince Ishmael*

5 Djuna Barnes *New York*

6 Arthur Schnitzler *Dream Story*

7 Susan Howe *The Europe of Trusts*

8 Gertrude Stein *Tender Buttons*

9 Arkadii Dragomoschenko *Description**

10 David Antin *Selected Poems: 1963-1973**

11 Lyn Hejinian *My Life***

12 F. T. Marinetti *Let's Murder the Moonshine: Selected Writings*

13 Heimito von Doderer *The Demons*

14 Charles Bernstein *Rough Trades**

15 Fanny Howe *The Deep North**

16 Tarjei Vesaas *The Ice Palace*

17 Jackson Mac Low *Pieces O' Six**

18 Steve Katz *43 Fictions**

19 Valery Larbaud *Childish Things**

20 Wendy Walker *The Secret Service**

21 Lyn Hejinian *The Cell**

22 Len Jenkin *Dark Ride and Other Plays**

23 Tom Raworth *Eternal Sections**

24 Ray DiPalma *Numbers and Tempers: Selected Poems**

25 Italo Svevo *As a Man Grows Older*

26 André Breton *Earthlight**

27 Fanny Howe *Saving History**

28 F. T. Marinetti *The Untameables*

29 Arkadii Dragomoschenko *Xenia**

30 Barbara Guest *Defensive Rapture**

31 Carl Van Vechten *Parties*

32 David Bromige *The Harbormaster of Hong Kong**

33 Keith Waldrop *Light While There is Light: An American History**

34 Clark Coolidge *The Rova Improvisations**

35 Dominique Fourcade *Xbo*\*
36 Marianne Hauser *Me & My Mom*\*
37 Arthur Schnitzler *Lieutenant Gustl*
38 Wilhelm Jensen/Sigmund Freud
*Gradiva/Delusion and Dream in* Gradiva
39 Clark Coolidge *Own Face*

\*First publication
\*\*Revised edition